Colourful Birds

by Claire Llewellyn

Contents

Birds and Colour

There are over 10,000 different kinds of birds in the world. Many of them have dull feathers of brown, grey or black. Some have very colourful feathers of blue, orange, yellow, red or green. This book explains why.

A sparrow has brown feathers.

A toucan is a very colourful bird.

A cuckoo's feathers are dull grey.

Did you know?

Birds are the only animals in the world to have feathers.

3

Sending Signals

Each kind of bird looks different. Birds use their colours and markings to tell other birds something about themselves. It's like sending a signal.

The signal might say, 'I'm the same **species** as you' or 'I'm female'.

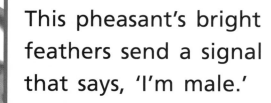

This pheasant's bright feathers send a signal that says, 'I'm male.'

Many birds grow different new feathers at certain times of the year. This sends a different signal. It might say, 'I'm an adult', 'I'm healthy' and 'Shall we have chicks?'

This male goldfinch turns golden when it's time for the female to have chicks.

Did you know?

Birds have very good eyesight. They see each other's signals clearly.

Roller

Rollers are beautiful birds with blue feathers. In the spring, the strongest birds have the brightest feathers and quickly **pair up** with one another.

Their feathers send a signal that says, 'I'm well fed because I'm good at hunting. I'll make a great parent and my chicks are more likely to survive.'

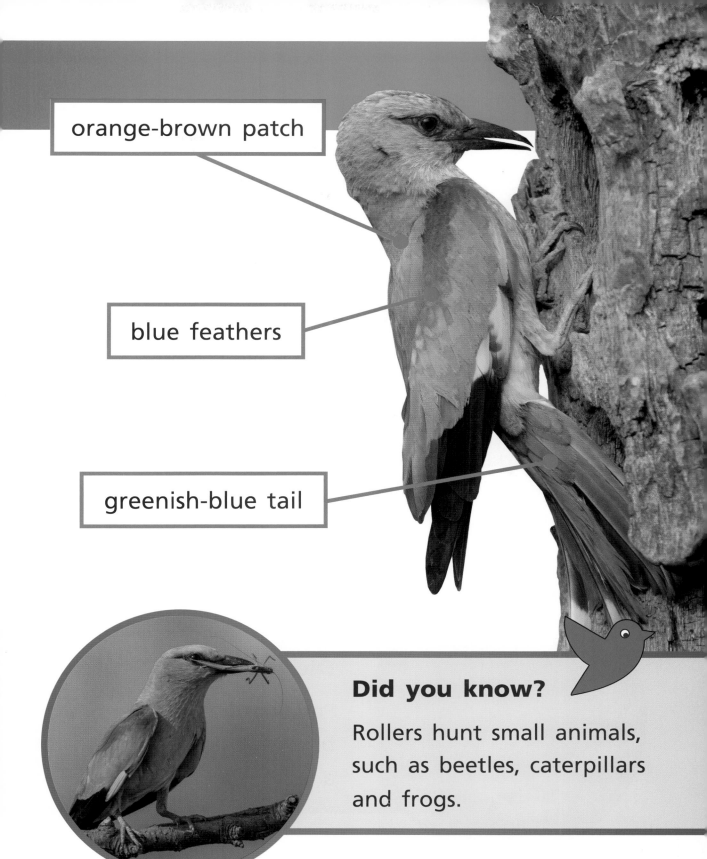

orange-brown patch

blue feathers

greenish-blue tail

Did you know?

Rollers hunt small animals, such as beetles, caterpillars and frogs.

7

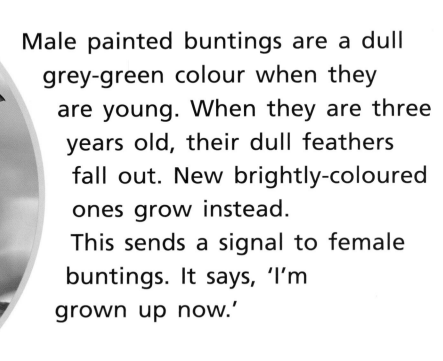

Male painted buntings are a dull grey-green colour when they are young. When they are three years old, their dull feathers fall out. New brightly-coloured ones grow instead.

This sends a signal to female buntings. It says, 'I'm grown up now.'

Did you know?

Female buntings are not brightly-coloured. They are a yellow-green colour.

bright blue head

red eye-ring

yellow-green on back

red breast

Hummingbird

Hummingbirds are tiny birds. They have brightly-coloured feathers that shimmer in the light. The male ruby-throated hummingbird grows red feathers on his throat when he is ready to start a family. He **displays** them to the females by lifting and turning his head.

dark green **crown**

ruby-red throat

grey breast

Did you know?

There are over 300 species of hummingbird. Each one has its own colours and markings.

Kingfisher

Kingfishers are river birds that hunt for fish.
Each male stays in his part of
the river to hunt.
If he sees another male,
the bird opens
his wings to display
his orange breast.

This gives a clear signal:
'Go away at once or
I will fight.'

Did you know?

Kingfishers pair up
in the spring. Some of them
pair for life.

greenish-blue feathers

orange bill

white throat patch

red leg

reddish-brown breast

13

Peacock

In the spring, peacocks grow long green tail feathers with bright eyespots. Peacocks lift their tails and shake them to show off to the female birds.

The female is called a peahen.

The peahens choose the peacock with the longest tail and the most eyespots.

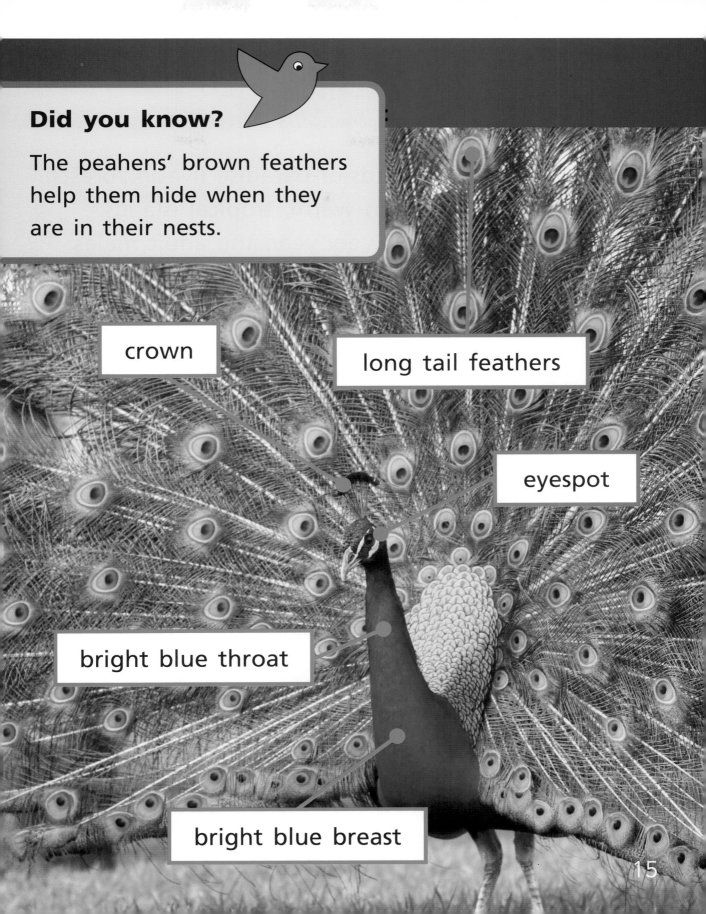

Did you know?

The peahens' brown feathers help them hide when they are in their nests.

crown

long tail feathers

eyespot

bright blue throat

bright blue breast

Bird-of-Paradise

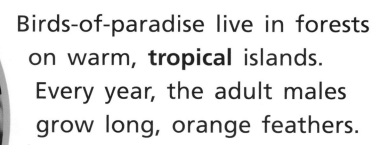

Birds-of-paradise live in forests on warm, **tropical** islands. Every year, the adult males grow long, orange feathers.

The males display their feathers to the females by dancing and bowing in the trees.

yellow eye

orange head

reddish-brown wings

long tail feathers

Did you know?

Males lose their show feathers when the females have laid their eggs.

Eclectus Parrot

Eclectus parrots live in tropical forests. Male birds look for food in the treetops. Their green feathers help to hide them from predators, such as owls and hawks. The females guard the nest hole. Their red and blue feathers send a strong signal to other birds. It says, 'This is my hole. Go away.'

bright orange
beak

red head
and throat

green feathers

red patch
under wing

blueish breast

Did you know?

It is very rare for a female
bird to be more colourful
than the male.

Flamingos

Flamingos are tall pink or orange birds that live by lakes and seas. These birds are colourful for a special reason. They feed on shellfish and tiny seaweed. Both foods contain a strong **pigment**, that turns flamingos pink.

black wing tips

deep pink wing

pink leg

yellow eye

pale pink feathers

Did you know?

Flamingos are grey when they hatch. They turn pink by the time they are two years old.

21

Glossary

displays – behaves in a way that sends a signal

crown – top of the head

pair up – when males and females come together to have chicks

pigment – strong natural colour found in some animals, plants or rocks

species - type of bird

tropical – in the warmest parts of the world

22

Index

Colourful Birds ✎ Claire Llewellyn

Teaching notes written by Sue Bodman and Glen Franklin

Using this book

Developing reading comprehension

Beautiful photographs feature in this text exploring how birds use colour to send signals. Non-fiction features, such as labels and captions, provide the context for children to locate specific information and read for information effectively. The glossary defines less commonly-used words and supports comprehension.

Grammar and sentence structure

- Adverbial phrases are used to modify the timing and frequency of the verb (e.g. 'When they are three years old' on p.8, 'In the spring' on p.6 and p.14).
- Direct speech is used in a novel way providing information about the purpose of the signals (e.g. 'a signal that says 'I'm well fed' on p.6).

Word meaning and spelling

- Subject-specific words are supported by the glossary and labelling.
- Bird names are often longer, multi-syllabic words ('Hummingbird'; 'Kingfisher', 'Eclectus Parrot') requiring attention to word detail.

Curriculum links

Science and Nature – Signals can draw attention to danger, to indicate their position, to create a diversion, to indicate fear or anger, or to create a relationship with an animal of the same species. Children could explore animal signals, researching questions such as Why do animals signal to each other? What do they use to create signals? They could create a display of common reasons for signalling and the animals who use them.

Drama – Have the children considered how challenging it is to communicate effectively without speech? Teach the class some simple sign language and use it to communicate. Play some games that require wordless communication, such as charades or the 'non-verbal introduction'.

Learning Outcomes

Children can:

- use the diagrams to extract specific simple information (i.e. colour)
- adapt to the different language styles employed in the text

- take note of punctuation and using it to keep track of longer sentences
- solve most unfamiliar words using appropriate word-reading strategies, and monitor that meaning is understood.

A guided reading lesson

Book Introduction

Give each child a copy of the book. In pairs, ask them to read the front cover and the blurb. Then ask them to quickly flick through and share their predictions of what type of book they think this is, giving reasons. Then discuss their predictions as a group, reinforcing the evidence for this being a non-fiction text.

Orientation

Turn to the title page and skim the contents. Ask: *Does this also help us to decide what type of book we are going to be reading today?* Remind children of the purposes for reading non-fiction, i.e. to find specific information related to topics of interest. Say: *Colour is very important in nature. Animals use colour to stay safe and to find other animals the same as them. In this book, we can find out why some birds are brightly coloured.* For younger children, it may be helpful to discuss birds common to the children's experience and establish which ones would be referred to as brightly-coloured and which would be regarded as dull or plain.

Preparation

Turn to the title page to look at the contents page. Read the birds' names aloud to the children, asking them to follow down through the list as you read. Which birds have they already heard of? What do they know about them? Model syllabification as a word-solving strategy for the longer multi-syllabic words, for example, 'hummingbird', 'kingfisher', 'flamingo'.

Pages 2 and 3: Ask the children to read page 2 quietly to themselves and then ask them to explain the difference between 'dull' and 'colourful'. Draw attention to the fact box entitled 'Did you know?' Tell the children to look out for the fact boxes as they read and explain that a fact box presents general information often not explained in the same way as the main text.

Pages 4 and 5: Read the heading 'Sending Signals'.